SCHOLASTIC

National Curriculu

ENGLISH

Revision Guide

✓ Recap
✓ Revise
✓ Skills Check

Ages 6-7
Year 2

KS1

SCHOLASTIC

National Curriculum
ENGLISH
Revision Guide

Book End, Range Road, Witney, Oxfordshire, OX29 0YD
Registered office: Westfield Road, Southam, Warwickshire CV47 0RA
www.scholastic.co.uk

5 6 7 8 9   8 9 0 1 2 3 4 5

British Library Cataloguing-in-Publication Data
A catalogue record for this book is available from the British Library.

ISBN 978-1407-15914-0
Printed in Malaysia

Author
Lesley and Graham Fletcher

Editorial
Rachel Morgan, Tracey Cowell, Helen Lewis, Shelley Welsh and Jane Jackson

Series Design
Scholastic Design Team: Nicolle Thomas and Neil Salt

Design
Oxford Designers & Illustrators

Cover Design
Scholastic Design Team: Nicolle Thomas and Neil Salt

Cover Illustration
Shutterstock / © VIGE.CO

Illustration
Matt Ward @ Beehive illustration

Contents

Reading

Using the revision guide

From 2016 new style National Curriculum Tests will be introduced for children at the end of Key Stage 1 (7 years old) and at the end of Key Stage 2 (11 years old).

• This book has been written to help children revise for the new style tests in Reading and in Grammar, Punctuation and Spelling at the end of Key Stage 1.

• This book is split into five sections, which match the content to be covered by the tests.

• Revising for the tests will help children feel prepared and prevent them from worrying about the unknown.

• Use this book to practise skills 'little and often'. Don't attempt to do too much in one session.

• A series of **Practice Tests** is available to help children towards the next stage of their preparations for National and school tests.

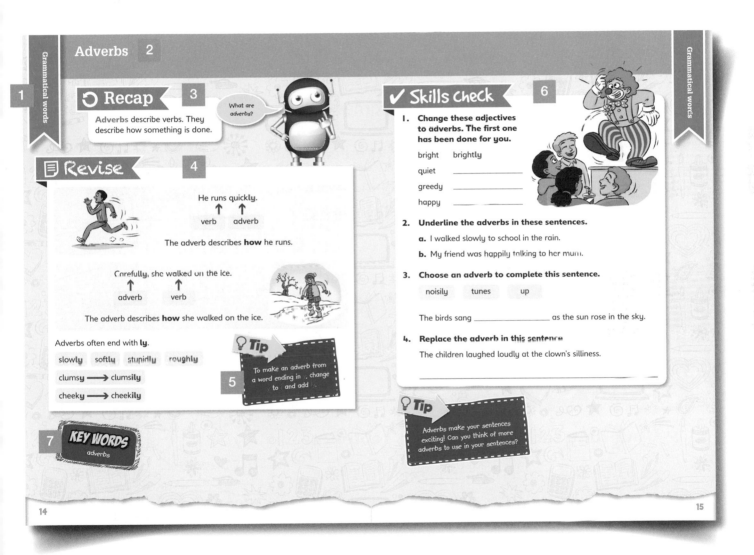

1 Chapter

2 Page title

3 Each page starts with a **recap**. A 'What is...' question is followed by a clear definition of the terminology used.

4 In the **revise** section there are clear teaching examples, using fun characters and clear illustrations and diagrams.

5 **Tips** are included to help show important points to remember and to give helpful strategies for remembering.

6 The **skills check** sections enable children to practise what they have learned using National Test-style questions.

7 **Key words** that children need to know are displayed. Definitions for these words can be found in the **Glossary**.

Nouns

↺ Recap

What are nouns?

Nouns are naming words.
Nouns name people, places and things.

📄 Revise

ball

beach   boy   ball

↑   ↑   ↑
names a place names a person names a thing

boy

Look at these **sentences**. The nouns are in bold.

The **children** bought some **sweets** in **town**.
I like going to the **zoo** to see the **elephants**.

beach

💡 Tip

A noun names something.

✔ Skills Check

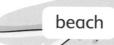

1. **Underline the nouns in each sentence.**

   a. I dug the garden with a spade.

   b. I ate pasta with a spoon.

2. **Choose a different noun to complete each sentence.**

   sun   day   girl   cat   night

   a. I walked through the dark _____.

   b. It was a cold, snowy _____.

KEY WORDS

nouns
sentences

Nouns with capital letters

Recap

Can nouns start with capital letters?

Some nouns start with **capital letters**.
These nouns name a particular person, place, day of the week or name of a month.

Revise

Nouns that name a particular person, place, a day of the week or month of the year start with a capital letter.

Names of people

Josh

Irena

Mrs Brown

$10 \times 2 =$
$20 \times 10 =$

Names of places

Blackpool

England

Africa

Blackpool

Names of days

Monday

Saturday

Wednesday

Go Shopping Saturday

Names of months

January

March

November

MARCH

KEY WORDS

capital letters

✔ Skills Check

1. **Underline the nouns that start with a capital letter.**

   a. We gave our homework to Mr Patel.

   b. Our class go swimming every Tuesday.

2. **Circle the nouns that should start with a capital letter.**

   a. I am going to menorca for my holiday.

   b. My birthday is in february.

   c. preston is on the river ribble.

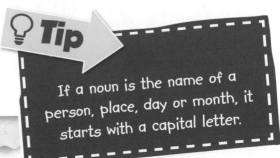

Tip

If a noun is the name of a person, place, day or month, it starts with a capital letter.

Adjectives

↻ Recap

What are adjectives?

Adjectives are describing words.
They describe what a noun is like.

🗎 Revise

Here is a noun: **house**. What is the house like?

a **new** house   a **large** house   a **spooky** house

These three adjectives describe very different houses!

✔ Skills Check

1. **Underline the adjectives in these sentences.**

   a. They had a windy walk home.

   b. A gigantic parcel arrived this morning.

KEY WORDS
adjectives

2. **Use an adjective to complete each sentence.**

   a. At last they found the _____ treasure chest.

   b. We couldn't wait to arrive at the _____ castle.

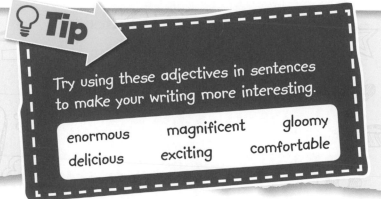

💡 Tip

Try using these adjectives in sentences to make your writing more interesting.

enormous	magnificent	gloomy
delicious	exciting	comfortable

Noun phrases

What are noun phrases?

↺ Recap

Noun phrases are groups of words that include a noun.

📄 Revise

A noun phrase can be made up of an adjective and a noun.

adjective + **noun** = noun phrase

a **windy day**

adjective + **noun** = noun phrase

the **kind teacher**

adjective + **noun** = noun phrase

💡 Tip

You can use more than one adjective to make your noun phrases even better!

the **cute, tabby** kitten

KEY WORDS

noun phrases

✔ Skills Check

1. **Circle the noun phrase in each sentence.**

   a. It was an interesting book.

   b. The train took us on a long, boring journey.

2. **Write a noun phrase to match each picture.**

a _____, _____ lion   the _____, _____ snake

Verbs: present tense

↺ Recap

What are verbs and what is the present tense?

Most **verbs** are doing words. They tell us what someone or something *does*.

Some verbs are being words. They tell us what someone or something *is*.

Verbs in the **present tense** describe actions that are happening now.

📄 Revise

KEY WORDS

verbs

present tense

These verbs all describe what someone is doing now.

he **sleeps**

she **writes**

they **walk**

These verbs are all being words.

I **am**   he **is**

you **are**

They are all written in the present tense.

✔ Skills Check

💡 Tip

Does the word tell us what someone or something is doing? If it does, it's a verb!

1. **Circle the verbs in each sentence.**

   a. Jack draws a picture of a train.

   b. They eat their sandwiches hungrily.

2. **Write each sentence in the present tense.**

   a. We looked in the shops for a football.

   _____

   b. She watched a very scary film.

   _____

Verbs: past tense

What is the past tense?

↺ Recap

Verbs in the **past tense** describe actions that have already happened.

🗐 Revise

Add **ed** to make the past tense of most verbs.

Present tense	Past tense
she cooks ⟶	she cook**ed**
I watch ⟶	I watch**ed**
we paint ⟶	we paint**ed**

Some verbs form their past tense differently. You do not add **ed**.

Present tense	Past tense
I drink ⟶	I drank
he sleeps ⟶	he slept
you buy ⟶	you bought

✔ Skills Check

1. **Write the correct verbs to complete the table.**

Present tense	Past tense
we clean	we _____
I _____	I helped
he talks	he _____
they _____	they pushed

Tip

Watch out! Not all verbs form the past tense by adding ed.

2. **Write each verb in the past tense.**

   a.　pull　We _____ the rope onto the boat.

   b.　eat　She _____ her meal slowly.

Verbs: tenses with 'ing'

What are tenses with 'ing'?

↺ Recap

Sometimes we need to describe actions that are still happening now, or that were happening in the past.

To do this we use a being verb with a doing verb ending in **ing**.

📄 Revise

We can describe actions in the **present** that **are** happening now.

To do this we use the being verbs **am**, **is** or **are** + the doing verb ending **ing**.

am		I **am jumping**
is	+ **doing verb** and **ing**	he **is jumping**
are		they **are jumping**

We can describe actions in the **past** that **were** happening.

To do this, we use the being verbs **was** and **were** + the doing verb ending **ing**.

was	+ **doing verb** and **ing**	I **was laughing**
were		they **were laughing**

✔ Skills Check

1. **Choose the correct verb to complete the sentence.**

   is   am   are

   Ellie _____ washing her hair tonight.

2. **These events have already happened. Write the correct verb to complete each sentence.**

   a. The children were _____ sandcastles.

   b. Jane was _____ her bike.

Verb changes

How do verbs change?

↻ Recap

Verbs change based on who the person or thing is doing the action.

Verbs change depending on whether the action is happening now or happened in the past.

📄 Revise

	Present tense (Happening now)	**Past tense** (Happened in the past)
Being verbs	I **am** it/he/she **is** we/you/they **are**	I **was** it/he/she **was** we/you/they **were**
Doing verbs	I **look** it/he/she **looks** we/you/they **look**	I **looked** it/he/she **looked** we/you/they **looked**

For doing verbs:

Present tense: Add an **s** for **it, she** or **he**.

Past tense: For most verbs, add **ed**.

💡 **Tip**

Learn how each doing verb changes.

✔ Skills Check

1. **Which sentences are correct? Tick two.**

   I is going to the park. ☐   She am reading the comic. ☐

   We are having our tea. ☐   I am giving mum a present. ☐

2. **This event is happening now. Write the correct form of the verb.**

   start   It _____ raining as we leave the house.

13

Adverbs

↻ Recap

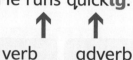

What are adverbs?

Adverbs describe verbs. They describe how something is done.

📄 Revise

He runs quick**ly**.

↑ verb ↑ adverb

The adverb describes **how** he runs.

Careful**ly**, she walked on the ice.

↑ adverb ↑ verb

The adverb describes **how** she walked on the ice.

Adverbs often end with **ly**.

slow**ly** soft**ly** stupid**ly** rough**ly**

clumsy ⟶ clums**ily**

cheeky ⟶ cheek**ily**

💡 Tip

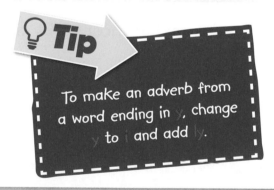

To make an adverb from a word ending in y, change y to i and add ly.

KEY WORDS
adverbs

✔ Skills Check

1. Change these adjectives to adverbs. The first one has been done for you.

bright   **brightly**

quiet   _____

greedy   _____

happy   _____

2. Underline the adverbs in these sentences.

a. I walked slowly to school in the rain.

b. My friend was happily talking to her mum.

3. Choose an adverb to complete this sentence.

noisily   tunes   up

The birds sang _____ as the sun rose in the sky.

4. Replace the adverb in this sentence.

The children laughed loudly at the clown's silliness.

_____

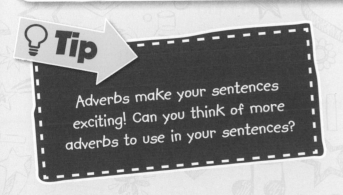

💡 **Tip**

Adverbs make your sentences exciting! Can you think of more adverbs to use in your sentences?

Joining words

What are joining words?

↻ Recap

Joining words join two words or two groups of words together.

📄 Revise

and   or   but

These are all joining words and can be used to join sentences or parts of sentences.

Here they join two sentences:

I am going to the beach **and** I will build a sandcastle.

Here they join two parts of sentences:

Would you like roast potatoes **or** would you like mashed?

I can dry the dishes **but** I can't wash them.

KEY WORDS
joining words

✔ Skills Check

1. **Write a different joining word to complete each sentence.**

    a. I dropped the plate _____ the mug.

    b. I wanted an egg _____ there were none left!

2. **Which joining word could complete this sentence? Tick one.**

    We could go to the zoo _____ we could go on a boat trip.

    and ☐   but ☐   or ☐

More joining words

What else do joining words do?

↻ Recap

Some joining words join extra information to a sentence.

📃 Revise

when	because	if	that

The end of the sentence gives extra information about the first part.

Joe walks the dog **when** he gets home from school.

Let me know **if** you would like a drink.

We went to a forest **that** has an adventure trail.

I didn't finish my homework **because** the baby was crying.

A joining word does not have to be in the middle of a sentence.

When it is my birthday, I will see my gran.

✔ Skills Check

1. **Underline the joining word in each sentence.**

   a. It was after dark when the owl began to hoot.

   b. If the car needs petrol, we will need to stop.

2. **Choose the <u>same</u> joining word to complete each sentence.**

   a. _____ I am eight years old, I will go into the next swimming group.

   b. They would have their tea _____ it was ready.

Sentence types: statements and questions

What are the different sentence types?

↻ Recap

There are four types of sentence: **statements**, **questions**, **exclamations** and **commands**.

🗒 Revise

All sentences start with a capital letter.

A **statement** states a fact. It ends with a **full stop**.

It is a red car.

I like ice cream.

A **question** asks a question. It ends with a **question mark**.

What time is it?

When will it be sunny?

💡 Tip

Questions often start with When, What, Which, Who, Why and How.

✔ Skills Check

1. **Match each sentence to the correct sentence type.**

Why did you go to the shops?	statement
It is a new house.	question
The dog is very muddy.	statement
Who wants a drink?	question

KEY WORDS

statements
questions
commands
exclamations

Sentence types: exclamations and commands

📄 Revise

An **exclamation** shows excitement, surprise or emotion.
It ends with an **exclamation mark**.

How fantastic**!**   What a scary film**!**

A **command** tells someone to do something.
It can end with an **exclamation mark** or a **full stop**.

Tidy up**!** ⟵ Forceful command.
Ends with an
exclamation mark.

Tidy up, please**.** ⟵ Not as forceful.
Ends with a full stop.

✔ Skills Check

I. **Tick the boxes to show the sentence types.**

Sentence	Statement	Question	Command	Exclamation
Go home				
How much has it grown				
How clever				
It was planted last week				

Apostrophes to show missing letters

How are apostrophes used?

↺ Recap

An **apostrophe** can be used in place of missing letters.

📄 Revise

When we join words together we use an apostrophe to show where letters have been missed out.

In these words, the apostrophe shows where the letter **o** has been missed out.

could n**o**t	did n**o**t	is n**o**t
↓	↓	↓
couldn't	didn't	isn't

Can you work out the missing letters in these joined words?

We can also use an apostrophe to join these words:

I am = I'm   it is = it's   we are = we're

they have = they've   here is = here's   we will = we'll

There are lots of others!

✔ Skills Check

KEY WORDS
apostrophes

1. **Join the words in bold using an apostrophe.**

   a. I **have not** got any money. _____

   b. We **cannot** reach it. _____

2. **Write these joined words in full.**

   a. I've _____   **c.** they're _____

   b. doesn't _____   **d.** what's _____

Apostrophes to show belonging

How else are apostrophes used?

↺ Recap

An apostrophe can also be used to show that something belongs to someone.

📄 Revise

We use an **apostrophe** + **s** to show that something belongs to someone.

Ellie**'s** book

↑
apostrophe + s

The book belongs to Ellie.

the dog**'s** ball

↑
apostrophe + s

The ball belongs to the dog.

Plurals do **not** need an apostrophe.

We ate a lot of Easter egg**s**.

💡 Tip

If it belongs to something or someone, it needs an apostrophe + s!

✔ Skills Check

I. Write an apostrophe in the correct place in each sentence.

a. We were woken up by the babys crying.

b. I enjoyed playing with my friends game.

2. Which sentences use apostrophes correctly? Tick two.

The cat's ate lots of food. ☐   The cat's food had been eaten. ☐

The cake's were all sold. ☐   The cake's filling was delicious. ☐

Commas in lists

How are commas used?

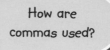

↻ Recap

Commas are used to separate items in a list.

📄 Revise

Use commas to separate a list of objects.

We used mango, strawberries, lime and apples to make a smoothie.

Use a comma after each item.   **Do not** use a comma before *and*.

Josh, Anwar, Omar, Tomas and Richard came to my party.

KEY WORDS

commas

Tip 💡

You need a comma after each item in a list.

Do not use a comma before and.

✔ Skills Check

1. Write commas in the correct places in these sentences.

a. I have a sandwich apple crisps and a drink in my lunch box.

b. September April June and November all have thirty days.

2. Which sentence uses commas correctly? Tick one.

The rescue centre helps dogs, cats, rabbits, and guinea pigs. ☐

Girls, and boys both like playing football cricket and, netball. ☐

My grandparents, cousins, aunts and uncles all came to my party. ☐

Prefixes

What is a prefix?

↻ Recap

A **prefix** is a set of letters you can put at the beginning of a word to change its meaning.

📑 Revise

un is a prefix.

If you put **un** before a word, it will mean the opposite.

kind ⟶ **un**kind
means **not** kind

happy ⟶ **un**happy
means **not** happy

like ⟶ **un**like
means **not** like

able ⟶ **un**able
means **not** able

✔ Skills Check

1. **Colour the prefix in each word.**

u	n	f	o	l	d

u	n	b	l	o	c	k

u	n	d	o

u	n	c	o	v	e	r

2. **Use a prefix to change each word to its opposite meaning.**

    a. _____ zip

    b. _____ usual

    c. _____ bolt

    d. _____ dress

💡 Tip

The prefix un means not. It changes a word to mean the opposite.

KEY WORDS

prefix

Suffixes

↻ Recap

What is a suffix?

A **suffix** is a set of letters you can put at the end of a word to change its meaning.

📄 Revise

Here are some suffixes:

| ness | less | ment | ful |

bright + **ness** = bright**ness**
adjective   *noun*

taste + **less** = taste**less**
noun   *adjective*

enjoy + **ment** = enjoy**ment**
verb   *noun*

care + **ful** = care**ful**
noun   *adjective*

To add a suffix to a word ending in **y**, change **y** to **i**.
plent**y** + **ful** = plent**iful**
noun   *adjective*

✔ Skills Check

1. **Underline the suffix in each word.**

    amazement

    handful

    penniless

    fondness

2. **Draw lines to join each word to a suffix to make a new word.**

move		ness
tear		less
hope		ment
sad		ful

💡 Tip

Adding a suffix changes the type of word. You can add more than one suffix:
care + ful + ly = carefully

KEY WORDS

suffix

Suffixes: 'er' and 'est'

🗏 Revise

er and **est** are suffixes. We use these suffixes to compare things.

tall	tall**er**	tall**est**
sad	sad**der**	sad**dest**

Sometimes you need to double the end letter before adding the suffix.

We can also add **er** to verbs to change them to nouns.

keep ⟶ keep**er**
verb   *noun*

teach ⟶ teach**er**
verb   *noun*

✔ Skills Check

1. **Which sentence uses suffixes correctly? Tick one.**

    It was the small kitten in the basket. ☐

    It was the smaller kitten in the basket. ☐

    It was the smallest kitten in the basket. ☐

2. **Add a suffix to each verb to change it into a noun.**

    clean_____   build_____

> 💡 **Tip**
>
> To compare two things, add er.
> I am bigger than my brother.
> To compare three or more things, add est.
> My brother is the biggest boy in his class.

25

Word families

What is a word family?

↺ Recap

A **word family** is a group of words that have similar letter patterns and meanings.

They often have the same **root word** but different beginnings and endings.

💡 **Tip**

Learn how to spell the root word. Then just add the prefix or suffix.

📄 Revise

poor is a root word. We can add suffixes to make new words:

poor**ly**   poor**er**   poor**est**

All these words belong to the same word family.

kind is a root word. We can add prefixes or suffixes to make new words:

unkind   kind**ly**   kind**er**

kind**est**   kind**ness**   **un**kind**ly**

All these words belong to the same word family.

✔ Skills Check

1. **Circle the word in each group that does <u>not</u> belong to the same word family.**

   a. enjoy   enjoyable   rejoined   unenjoyable   enjoyed

   b. hopeless   hopping   hopeful   hopefully   hoping

2. **Write one more word for each word family.**

   a. happy   happier   _____

   b. sad   sadly   _____

KEY WORDS

word families

root word

Word families: verbs

↻ Recap

What are verb word families?

We use different forms of verbs depending on **who** is doing the action and **when** the action is happening.

The different forms of a verb belong to the same word family.

📋 Revise

Climb is the root word.

| I climb | she climb**s** |

| she is climb**ing** | she climb**ed** |

Climb, **climbs**, **climbing** and **climbed** are all in the same word family.

Dive is the root word.

| I dive | he dive**s** |

| he is div**ing** | he div**ed** |

Dive, **dives**, **diving** and **dived** are all in the same word family.

💡 Tip

To add ing or ed to a root word ending in e, take off the e first.

✔ Skills Check

1. **Choose the correct form of the verb to complete the sentence.**

   | move | moves | moving | moved |

   He is _____ house next week.

2. **Complete the table with the correct verb forms for the verb 'drip'.**

Present tense	Past tense
I drip	I _____
he _____	it _____
we are _____	they _____

Long vowel sounds

What is a long vowel sound?

↻ Recap

The **vowels** are the letters **a**, **e**, **i**, **o** and **u**.

A **long vowel sound** is a sound which sounds like the letter's name.

📄 Revise

There are many ways to make one sound.

Long a sound	Long e sound	Long i sound	Long o sound	Long u sound
make day rain	these feet field read	five night pie	home road bowl	tube new

💡 Tip

Try to learn spellings in groups like these.

night	field	road	brain
fight	chief	toad	paid
sight	grief	coach	afraid
delight	thief	goal	wait

✔ Skills Check

1. **Underline all the long e sounds.**

   a. We went to the beach to see the sand.

   b. The chief raised the green flag completely.

2. **Circle the correct spelling for each word.**

   a. frite   friet   fright

   b. cube   cewb   cueb

   c. sheeld   shield   sheald

KEY WORDS

vowels

long vowel sound

Tricky vowel sounds: 'or' and 'air'

What is tricky about the vowel sounds or and air?

↻ Recap

The vowel sounds **or** and **air** can be tricky because they can be spelled in lots of different ways.

📄 Revise

or	au	ore	aw	oor
for	caught	more	saw	door
short	author	score	jaw	poor
born	August	before	yawn	floor

air	ere
fair	there
stair	where
chair	nowhere

are	ear
bare	bear
fare	wear
scared	pear

Some of these words sound the same, but have a different spelling.

fair

fare

Different spelling = different meaning

✔ Skills Check

1. **Circle the bold words that are spelled correctly.**

   a. My teacher **tort / taught / tawt** me about Florence Nightingale.

   b. **Dinosores / dinosaws / dinosaurs** lived millions of years ago.

   c. My little sister has begun to **crorl / craul / crawl**.

2. **Underline the bold words that are spelled correctly.**

   a. I cuddle my teddy **bear / bare** in bed.

   b. We picked **pairs / pears** off the tree.

   c. He went **upstairs / upstares** to fetch his book.

💡 Tip

Be careful! The letters ear can make a different sound, as in wear and fear.

29

Tricky letter pairs: 'kn', 'wh' and 'wr'

↻ Recap

What is tricky about kn, wh and wr?

These pairs of letters are tricky because one letter in each pair is a **silent letter**.

A silent letter is a letter you can't hear when you say the word.

📄 Revise

kn	wh	wr
silent **k**	silent **h**	silent **w**
know	**wh**en	**wr**ist
knee	**wh**at	**wr**ong
knot	**wh**ich	**wr**ap

💡 **Tip**

To help spell these words, sound-out the silent letter.

KEY WORDS

silent letter

✔ Skills Check

1. **Colour the silent letter in each word.**

w	r	i	t	e

k	n	o	b

w	h	o	l	e

k	n	i	f	e

2. **Read the clues and write the words. Spell each word correctly.**

Clues	Words
To use needles and wool to make clothes	_____
A ship at the bottom of the sea	_____
To bang on the door	_____
The opposite of black	_____

Tricky letter pairs: 'ph' and 'qu'

What is tricky about ph and qu?

↺ Recap

ph and **qu** can be tricky because they make sounds like other letters.

📋 Revise

ph makes a **f** sound as in fan.

ele**ph**ant

tele**ph**one

qu makes a **kw** sound.

q and **u** always go together!

queen

quarter

💡 Tip

p + h = f sound
q always goes with u

✔ Skills check

1. **Write a word that has qu or ph in each space.**

    The dog ran _____ through the woods.

    In the _____ g comes after f.

2. **Use each of these words in a sentence.**

    a. graph _____

    _____

    b. quiet _____

    _____

31

Tricky endings: 'le' or 'el', 'al' or 'il'?

What is tricky about these endings?

↻ Recap

The endings **le**, **el**, **al** and **il** all sound the same, so it can be tricky to know which one to use.

🗒 Revise

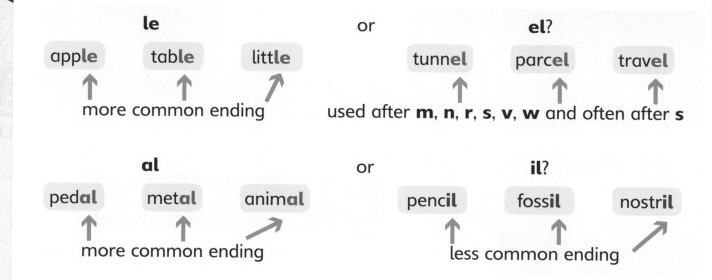

le   or   **el**?

apple	table	little

↑ ↑ ↑
more common ending

tunnel	parcel	travel

↑ ↑ ↑
used after **m, n, r, s, v, w** and often after **s**

al   or   **il**?

pedal	metal	animal

↑ ↑ ↗
more common ending

pencil	fossil	nostril

↑ ↑ ↗
less common ending

💡 Tip

Say each word and exaggerate the end sound to help you learn the spelling.

tab-le   tunn-el
met-al   penc-il

Remember: le and al are the most common endings.

✔ Skills Check

1. **Circle the correct spelling for each word.**

   a. camle   camel   camal   camil

   b. capital   capitil   capetal   capitel

   c. squirral   sqirrel   squirrle   squirrel

2. **Match each beginning to the correct ending to make a word.**

tow	hospit	bott	pup

le	il	el	al

Tricky endings: 'dge' or 'ge'?

↻ Recap

What is tricky about these endings?

The endings **dge** and **ge** sound the same, so it can be tricky to know which one to use.

📋 Revise

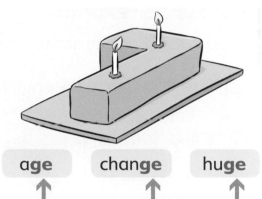

ledge	fudge	bridge
↑	↑	↑

Use **dge** after a **short vowel sound**.

short vowel sounds:

a as in c**a**t	**e** as in **e**gg	**i** as in b**i**n

o as in c**o**t	**u** as in b**u**t

age	change	huge
↑	↑	↑

Use **ge** after all other sounds.

💡 Tip

Never use j at the end of a word.

✔ Skills check

1. **Write the dge and ge words in the correct part of the table.**

ledge	page	badge	charge	dodge

after a short vowel sound	after all other sounds

2. **Underline the correct spelling of each word.**

   a. stage / stadge

   b. lardge / large

   c. strange / strandge

   d. juge / judge

Tricky words

What are tricky words?

↻ Recap

Tricky words may be longer words or words with unusual spelling patterns.

📄 Revise

Tricky words are easier to spell if we split them into parts.

children = child + ren ⟵ Learn **ild** in ch**ild**.

everybody = every + body ⟵ There is **very** in e**very**.

beautiful = beauty + ful ⟵ Change end **y** to **i**. Add **ful**.
Learn **eau** in b**eau**ty.

✔ Skills Check

1. **Fill in the table.**

Word	Split into parts	Unusual spelling patterns
friendly		
behind		
improve		
people		

2. **Use each of these words in a sentence.**

   a. others _____

   b. because _____

   c. clothes _____

Compound words

Recap

What are compound words?

Compound words are made up of two or more other words.

Tip

To make a compound word easier to spell, split it into the words that make it up.

Revise

Two or more words can be put together to make one new word.

motor + way = motorway

book + shelf = bookshelf

fire + work = firework

snow + man = snowman

✔ Skills Check

1. **Draw lines to join each word with another to make a compound word.**

tooth	fish
rain	glasses
sun	brush
jelly	coat

2. **Write a different word after each word to make a compound word.**

a. moon_____

b. wheel_____

c. tea_____

d. bed_____

KEY WORDS
compound words

Words that sound the same

↻ Recap

What are words that sound the same?

Some words sound the same but are spelled differently and have different meanings.

💡 Tip

When words sound the same you need to work out what each one means. That might help you work out how it is spelled.

📄 Revise

These words all sound the same but have different spellings.

there	**their**	**they're**
There is a dog.	We have **their** books.	**They're** coming for tea.
↑	↑	↑
where it is	belonging to them	they are

here	**hear**
Here is my story.	I can **hear** a bird singing.
↖	↑
where it is	sense sounds
here is hiding in w**here**	**ear** is hiding in h**ear**

✔ Skills Check

1. **Choose the correct word to complete each sentence.**

   there   they're   their

   a. Look over _____!

   b. Have you wrapped _____ presents?

   c. I don't know if _____ here yet.

More words that sound the same

📄 Revise

its

The spider is in **its** web
↑
belonging to it

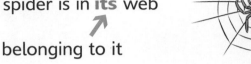

it's

It's a spider!
↑
short for *it is*

wear

You must **wear** gloves.
↑
put on

where

Where did you put your gloves?
↑
question word about position

ate

I **ate** a large pizza.
↑
had food

eight

A spider has **eight** legs.
↑
a number

✔ Skills check

1. **Circle the correct bold word in each sentence.**

   a. There is a **sale** / **sail** on in our local bike shop.

   b. Jack went to **meat** / **meet** his friend.

   c. The dog hurt his **poor** / **pore** / **paw**.

2. **Write a sentence using each word.**

   a. sun _____

   _____

   b. son _____

   _____

Plurals with 's' and 'es'

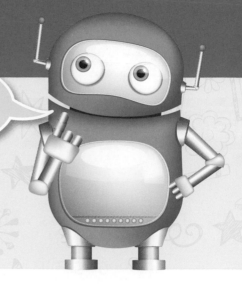

What is a plural?

↻ Recap

A **plural** is when there is more than one of something.

📄 Revise

For most **singular** words, just add **s** to make them plural.

Singular		Plural
one desk	→	two desk**s**
the school	→	many school**s**
a hat	→	several hat**s**

Some singular words end in **x**, **ch**, **sh**, **s**, **ss**, or **z**.
Add **es** to make these words plural.

Singular		Plural
the box	→	many box**es**
one beach	→	several beach**es**
a wish	→	three wish**es**

✔ Skills Check

1. **Write the singular or plural of these words.**

Singular	Plural
window	
kiss	
	churches
	flowers
	toes

💡 **Tip**

If it sounds like *s* or *z* at the end, it ends in *s*.
If it sounds like *iz* at the end, it ends in *es*.

KEY WORDS
plural
singular

Other plurals

📋 Revise

Some singular words end in **y**.
To make these words plural, change **y** to **i** and add **es**.

Singular		Plural
one fair**y**	→	two fair**ies**
a bab**y**	→	many bab**ies**
the famil**y**	→	some famil**ies**

If a word ends in **ay**, **ey**, **iy**, **oy** or **uy**, just add **s**.

Singular		Plural
one boy	→	two boy**s**
a donkey	→	three donkey**s**
the toy	→	many toy**s**

✔ Skills Check

1. **Write the plural of each word.**

   a. tray _____

   d. key _____

   b. lady _____

   e. fly _____

   c. lorry _____

   f. berry _____

2. **Write the plural of each word in brackets to complete the sentences.**

   a. Lots of _____ (turkey) are sold at Christmas.

   b. We walked through several _____ (valley) before reaching the village.

   c. Some _____ (country) are often hot.

What words mean

↻ Recap

How do we know what words mean?

Sometimes when you are reading, you come across a word you don't understand. You can use what you know already to work out what the word means.

📄 Revise

Last night's firework display was an electrifying event that thrilled thousands of people.

What does **electrifying** mean in this sentence?

Read the whole sentence and look for clues.

Last night's firework **display** was an **electrifying** event that **thrilled** thousands of people.

unknown word clues

Use the clues to help you work out what the unknown word means.

A **display** is something you watch or look at.

Thrilled means excited.

So in this sentence, **electrifying** might mean *exciting to watch*.

Another way to work out what the word means is to see if it looks like a word you already know.

Electrifying looks like electric or electricity. Electricity is used for lights. It can cause large sparks. In this sentence electrifying might mean having lots of bright lights or sparks.

So, in this piece of writing, electrifying means exciting to watch or full of bright lights.

✔ Skills Check

> The wind blew fiercely across the field.

1. Which word tells us that the wind was blowing very strongly?

_____

> Leaves were shredded from the trees.

2. In this sentence, *shredded* means:

Tick **one**.

taken ☐   hanging ☐   ripped ☐   floating ☐

> Suddenly, the storm stopped as briskly as it had started.

3. What does the word *briskly* mean in this sentence?

_____

💡 **Tip**

If you don't know what a word means, read the whole sentence and see if you can work it out.

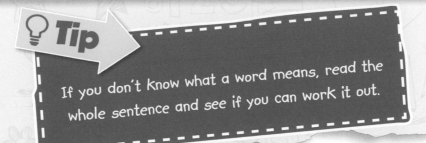

Ordering events

↺ Recap

What does ordering events mean?

Events are things that happen in a piece of writing. You need to be able to find events and put them in the order that they happen.

📄 Revise

Ralf's first day

It was Ralf's first day at school. **He walked up the drive with his mother.** As soon as **they started to cross the playground,** Ralf saw lots of bigger boys and girls.

← 1st event

← 2nd event
← 3rd event

Here are the events in order:

1. He walked up the drive with his mother.
2. They started to cross the playground.
3. Ralf saw lots of bigger boys and girls.

✔ Skills Check

Read the next part of Ralf's story.

Some of the children started running around near him. It became very noisy. Ralf held his mother's hand tightly. As the teacher met them at the door, she was smiling. She looked friendly. Ralf thought that everything would be all right.

1. **Draw lines to order the events.**

The teacher met them at the door. | 1 |

Ralf held his mother's hand tightly. | 2 |

Some of the children started running around near Ralf. | 3 |

Reading

42

Explaining the order of events

↺ Recap

What does it mean to explain the order of events?

When you explain the order of events, you say why things happened in the order they did.

🗐 Revise

In this story, the events are numbered for you.

Juggling

(1) My dad bought my sister, Anna, some juggling balls and a book on how to juggle for her sixth birthday. (2) By the time she was seven she had given up using them. It was far too hard. (3) For Anna's next birthday, Dad gave her a DVD on how to juggle. That made it much easier.

Explain why Anna's dad bought her a DVD for her seventh birthday.

This question is about the 3rd event. Look at the 1st and 2nd events to work out the answer.

Anna's dad bought her a DVD because she had tried using a book but it was too hard so she had given up.

✔ Skills Check

Read the next part of the story.

Soon Anna could juggle with three balls. It took her another year to be able to do it with four. By then it was easy, so she tried with much more difficult things like bottles and cups. She had to stop using the cups, as she broke so many we didn't have enough left to drink from!

1. **Why did Anna use bottles and cups after the juggling balls?**

_____

_____

How texts are organised

How are texts organised?

Texts can be organised in many different ways. Writers organise their texts to make them easier to read.

✎ Revise

Ways of organising texts include headings, subheadings, numbers and bullet points.

heading: tells you what the whole piece of writing is about

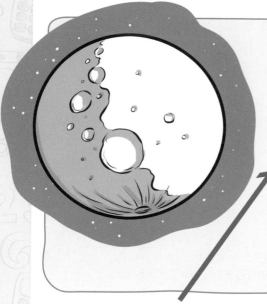

The Moon

People have watched the Moon since the beginning of time. Many people have dreamed of going there, but only a few have been.

Walking on the Moon

The first person to walk on the Moon was Neil Armstrong in 1969. He landed there with Buzz Aldrin. The last person walked on the moon in December 1972. No one has been there since.

subheading: tells you the particular thing this part of the writing is about

heading: tells you what the whole piece of writing is about

numbers: tell you the order things are done

Boiling water in a kettle

1. Put enough water in the kettle.
2. Plug the kettle in.
3. Switch the kettle on.
4. Wait for the water to boil.

Shopping list ← **heading:** tells you what the whole piece of writing is about

- 3 onions
- A litre of milk
- Teabags ← **bullet points:** tell you what is needed, but not the order
- Flowers

✔ Skills Check

1. In *The Moon*, what ways are used to organise the text?

Tick **two**.

headings ☐   bullet points ☐

numbers ☐   subheadings ☐

2. Draw lines to match each way of organising a text to what it tells you.

Way of organising a text

| headings |
| subheadings |
| numbers |
| bullet points |

What it tells you

| the order things are done |
| what the whole piece of writing is about |
| what is needed, but not the order |
| what a part of the writing is about |

3. Which text uses bullet points? _____

4. Look at *Boiling water in a kettle*. Why does this text have numbers rather than bullet points?

Titles

↻ Recap

Titles are like headings. They do the same job.

🖹 Revise

What would be a good title for this piece of writing?

> Grass is green. It grows very easily. All it needs are sun and rain. Lots of people have it in their gardens.

What is the writing all about? The answer is **'grass'**.

This reason **explains** why it is Grass is a good title

> A good title would be Grass. **Grass is in every sentence** but you might not know that because it is often called 'it'.

The title of this piece of writing is The night. Why is this a good title?

> ### The Night
>
> It's dark and it's cold
> But the moon shines so bright
> Making the world gold
> Even though it is night.

The moon comes out at night →

Tells us what the night is like

Tells us the time of day

It is a good title because each line tells us something about the night.

What would be another good title?

You could call the poem The Moon because three of the lines tell us about the moon and what it is doing.

✔ Skills Check

1. **Why would *Running* be a good title for this piece of writing?**

   > Running is a great hobby. It doesn't cost you anything and it keeps you fit.

   _____

2. **What would be a good title for this piece of writing?**

   > Over the hills and far away
   > There's a place called Mandalay
   > There sun shines every day
   > I wish I was in Mandalay.

   _____

3. **Why would your title be a good one?**

   _____

4. **This piece of writing could be called Deep in the Jungle or Exploring the Amazon.**

   Choose one title and explain why you think it is a good one.

   > All around me were huge trees, reaching to the sky for light. I moved through the Amazon rainforest, pushing through the thick undergrowth. Ahead of me, through the trees, I could see a fast-flowing river. It was a long way off but I knew that it must be the mighty Amazon itself.

   _____

   _____

Characters and events

↻ Recap

What are characters and events?

Characters are people in stories.
Events are things that happen in stories.

📄 Revise

character   **event**   **event**
↓   ↓   ↓

Curtis was **walking to school** when he saw **the car run into the bus**.
The **bus driver** got out and **looked at the damage** ← event
        ↑

Sometimes the character does not have a name.

✔ Skills check

Bella, Cheryl and Donna jumped off the bus and ran past the bus driver.

1. **Find and copy the characters in this sentence.**

_____

Donna and Cheryl stayed to help the driver while Bella called an ambulance.

2. **Find and copy two events from this sentence.**

1. _____

2. _____

Information

> What is information in writing?

↺ Recap

The information in a piece of writing is the ideas it contains.

▤ Revise

All these pieces of information tell us facts.

↓

Ben Nevis is **not a person**. It is a **mountain in Scotland**. It is **the tallest mountain in Britain**.

Ben Nevis is **very hard to climb. I was really tired** at the top. **I was glad to get down**.

↑

All these pieces of information tell us what someone thinks or how they felt.

> **💡 Tip**
>
> Information is often fact, but it can also be what someone thinks or feels.

✔ Skills Check

Shannon is a town in Ireland. It is named after a nearby river and it has an airport.

1. Find and copy two pieces of information from this piece of writing.

1. _____

2. _____

I like snakes. They aren't cold and slimy. They are warm and dry.

2. What information does this piece of writing contain? Tick two.

A lot of people like snakes. ☐   Snakes are cold and slimy. ☐

The writer likes snakes. ☐   Snakes are warm and dry. ☐

Explaining characters and events

What does it mean to explain characters and events?

↻ Recap

Explain means to say **why** or **how**. You have to give **reasons**.

📄 Revise

Characters You have to be able to explain what characters are like or why they do things.

Adele was **angry**. She had **lost her phone**
        ↑   ↑
  what Adele **is like**   the **reason** why

Events You have to be able to explain why something happened.

event   reason
  ↓   ↓
Dad checked the petrol in the car. It was **nearly empty**, so **he went to the garage** to fill it up.
            ↑
          event

The **reason** explains why the second event happened.

✔ Skills Check

Nasreen is very funny. She makes everyone laugh. We are all happy when Nasreen is here.

1. **Why does everyone like Nasreen?**

_____

Amina always went to the supermarket on Sunday mornings because it was quiet.

2. **Why did Amina always go to the supermarket on Sunday mornings?**

_____

Explaining information

↺ Recap

> What does it mean to explain information?

Explain means to say **why** or **how**.
You have to give **reasons**.

🗐 Revise

You have to be able to explain the reason for a piece of information.

In the Arctic, the **ice is melting**. This means **polar bears are in danger**.

reason   information

Why are the polar bears in danger? Because the ice is melting.

✔ Skills check

Tigers are good at hunting.
They can run fast and have
sharp claws and teeth.

1. **Why are tigers good at hunting?**

_____

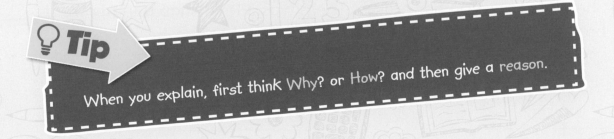

💡 Tip

When you explain, first think Why? or How? and then give a reason.

51

Predicting what might happen

↺ Recap

How do you predict what might happen?

You **guess** what will take place next.

You **use what you have read** to help you guess.

Revise

To predict, you need to read the whole text and then say what might happen next. In this text, the clues have been **highlighted**.

> Sam looked at the clock. **Only three minutes** to catch the bus! He put his coat on, but **it took him a long time to do the zip**. When he went out, **the key wouldn't work** to lock the door. He ran down the street but **tripped up and fell on the floor.**

Sam is trying to catch the bus. Do you think he will make it?

Clues	What the clues tell us
He only had three minutes. →	He hasn't got long to catch the bus.
His zip took a long time. →	The zip slows him down.
The key wouldn't work. →	The key slows him down more.
He fell on the floor. →	Falling over will slow him down even more.

The clues tell us: Sam is not likely to catch the bus because he will run out of time.

✔ Skills Check

1. **Colour the clues in the text that tell you what might happen next.**

> Lorna was going very fast on her bike. She needed to stop quickly. She pulled hard on her brakes. There was a loud snap and her front brake fell off!

2. **What do you think might happen next?**

_____

Making inferences

How do you make inferences?

↺ Recap

You work out what has happened.

You give a reason **why** you think it has happened.

📄 Revise

Ethan put his hand in his pocket to get the money to pay for his sweets. There was nothing there! He had put a pound coin in his pocket before he left home, but it wasn't there any more.

We know what has happened. Ethan had a pound coin in his pocket but he doesn't have it any more.

We don't know **why** he hasn't got it, so we have to guess.

The pound coin could:

- have fallen out of Ethan's pocket.
- have been stolen.
- have fallen through a hole in the pocket.
- still be there but Ethan just can't find it.
- have gone through a hole in the pocket and be stuck in the lining.

We don't know!

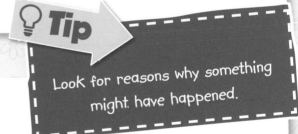

💡 **Tip**

Look for reasons why something might have happened.

✔ Skills check

Read the next part of Ethan's story.

Ethan felt in his pocket again and was surprised when his finger went all the way through and out of the other side.

1. **What do you think has happened to the pound coin?**

_____

2. **Give a reason for the answer you wrote for question 1.**

_____

Rhyme

What do you need to know about words and sounds?

↺ Recap

You need to be able to find:

- rhyming words.

📄 Revise

Words that have the same end sound **rhyme** with one another.

The sea was blue and grey and **green** ← **These words rhyme.**

It was the best I'd ever **seen** ←

Say the words out loud to see how they sound. If they sound almost the same, they rhyme.

✔ Skills check

1. **Circle the words that rhyme in each sentence.**

   a. Cats can walk but they really can't talk.

   b. Dogs are fun because they can run.

2. **Draw lines to match the words that rhyme.**

house	road
follow	scare
flowed	hollow
dare	mouse

Repeated sounds

What do you need to know about words and sounds?

↺ Recap

You need to be able to find:
- repeated sounds.

📋 Revise

In this sentence, some sounds are repeated:

The snake **sl**ithered, **sl**id and **sl**ipped through the long grass.

The **sl** sound is repeated.

✔ Skills Check

I. **Find and copy four words that repeat the same sound in this sentence.**

The rapid runners raced ahead as they ran towards the finish.

_____   _____

_____   _____

Words that describe sounds

What do you need to know about words and sounds?

📄 Revise

You might have to find words that describe sounds.

The rain **crashed** and **thumped** and **smashed** on the tin roof of the hut.

These words describe the sound the rain made.

✔ Skills Check

1. **In this sentence, the word *crackled* describes what the fire sounded like. Find and copy two other words that describe the sound of the fire.**

   The fire crackled loudly, then popped and whooshed as the flames went into the sky.

   _____ _____

💡 Tip

Look for words that sound like the noise they make, like crashed, banged or clanged.

Glossary

A

Adjectives are sometimes called 'describing words' because they pick out features of nouns such as size or colour. They can be used before or after a noun. The red bus.

Adverbs can describe the manner, time, place or cause of something. They tell you more information about the event or action.

Apostrophes:
show the place of missing letters (contraction).
show who or what something belongs to (possession).

B

Bullet points look this • and are used to list things. Bullet points tell you what you need, or what you need to do, but they do not tell you the order.

C

Capital letters are A, B, C, D, E, F, G, H, I, J, K, L, M, N, O, P, Q, R, S, T, U, V, W, X, Y and Z.

Commands are sentences that tell someone to do something, such as Please wash your hands. Commands may end with a full stop or an exclamation mark.

Commas look like this , and are used to separate items in a list, such as We took sandwiches, crisps, fruit and water on the picnic.

Compound words contain at least two root words. Some compound words are whiteboard, Superman.

E

Exclamations are sentences that show excitement, surprise or emotion, such as What a great surprise! Exclamations always end with an exclamation mark.

J

Joining words join two words or two groups of words together. Joining words include and, because, or, but, when, if and that.

L

Long vowel sound is a sound which sounds like the name of the letter: A, E, I, O, or U.

N

Nouns are naming words. They name people, places and things. Josh, boy, beach, England, ball and elephant are all nouns.

Noun phrases are groups of words that include a noun, such as a tall, thin man. Noun phrases may contain one or more adjectives.

P

past tense verbs describe past events. Most verbs take the suffix ed to form their past tense.

plural means 'more than one'.

prefix is a set of letters added to the beginning of a word in order to turn it into another word.

present tense verbs describe actions that are happening now.

Q

questions are sentences that ask a question, such as How old are you? Questions always end with a question mark.

R

root word is a word to which new words can be made by adding prefixes and suffixes: happy – unhappy – happiness.

S

sentences are groups of words which make sense on their own. All sentences start with a capital letter.

silent letter is a letter that does not make a sound when you read a word aloud.

singular means only one.

statements are sentences that state a fact, such as It is four o'clock.

suffix is a word ending or a set of letters added to the end of a word to turn it into another word.

V

verbs are doing and being words. They describe what is happening in a sentence. Verbs come in different tenses.

vowels are the letters a, e, i, o and u.

W

word families are normally related to each other by a combination of letter pattern, grammar and meaning: child – children – childish – childlike.

Word lists
These are the words you need to learn to spell.

Year 1

the	are	your	go	come	push
a	were	they	so	some	pull
do	was	be	by	one	full
to	is	he	my	once	house
today	his	me	here	ask	our
of	has	she	there	friend	
said	I	we	where	school	
says	you	no	love	put	

Year 2

door	climb	even	class	sugar	people
floor	most	great	grass	eye	water
poor	only	break	pass	could	again
because	both	steak	plant	should	half
find	old	pretty	path	would	money
kind	cold	beautiful	bath	who	Mr
mind	gold	after	hour	whole	Mrs
behind	hold	fast	move	any	parents
child	told	last	prove	many	Christmas
children	every	past	improve	clothes	
wild	everybody	father	sure	busy	

Answers: Year 2

GRAMMATICAL WORDS

Page 6

1 **a.** I dug the garden with a spade.
b. I ate pasta with a spoon.

2 **a.** I walked through the dark **night.**
b. It was a cold, snowy **day.**

Page 7

1 **a.** We gave our homework to Mr Patel.
b. Our class go swimming every Tuesday.

2 **a.** I am going to menorca for my holiday.
b. My birthday is in february.
c. preston is on the river ribble.

Page 8

1 **a.** They had a windy walk home.
b. A gigantic parcel arrived this morning.

2 Accept any appropriate adjective, for example:
a. At last they found the **old** treasure chest.
b. We couldn't wait to arrive at the **ruined** castle.

Page 9

1 **a.** It was an interesting book.
b. The train took us on a long, boring journey.

2 Accept any appropriate noun phrases, for example:
a **large**, **fierce** lion; the **long**, **curvy** snake.

Page 10

1 **a.** Jack draws a picture of a train.
b. They eat their sandwiches hungrily.

2 **a.** We look in the shops for a football.
b. She watches a very scary film.

Page 11

1

Present tense	Past tense
we clean	we **cleaned**
I **help**	I helped
he talks	he **talked**
they **push**	they pushed

2 **a.** We **pulled** the rope onto the boat.
b. She **ate** her meal slowly.

Page 12

1 Ellie **is** washing her hair tonight.

2 Alfie was **building** sandcastles.
Jane was **riding** her bike.

Page 13

1 We are having our tea.
I am giving mum a present.

2 It **starts** raining as we leave the house.

Page 15

1 quiet – **quietly**; greedy – **greedily**; happy – **happily**

2 **a.** I walked slowly to school in the rain.
b. My friend was happily talking to her mum.

3 The birds sang **noisily** as the sun rose in the sky.

4 Accept any appropriate adverb, for example
The children laughed **madly** at the clown's silliness.

Page 16

1 I dropped the plate **and** the mug.
I wanted an egg **but** there were none left!

2 or

Page 17

1 **a.** It was after dark when the owl began to hoot.
b. If the car needs petrol, we will need to stop.

2 When/because

PUNCTUATION

Page 18

1
Why did you go to the shops? → **question**
It is a new house. → **statement**
The dog is very muddy. → **statement**
Who wants a drink? → **question**

Page 19

1

Sentence	Statement	Question	Command	Exclamation
Go home			✓	
How much has it grown		✓		
How clever				✓
It was planted last week	✓			

Page 20

1 **haven't**
can't

2 **a.** I have **c.** they are
b. does not **d.** what is/what has

Page 21

1 **a.** We were woken up by the baby**'**s crying.
b. I enjoyed playing with my friend**'**s game.

2 The cat's food had been eaten.
The cake's filling was delicious.

Page 22

1 **a.** I have a sandwich**,** apple**,** crisps and a drink in my lunch box.
b. September**,** April**,** June and November all have thirty days.

2 My grandparents, cousins, aunts and uncles all came to my party.

VOCABULARY

Page 23

1 **un**fold **un**block **un**do **un**cover

2 **a. un**zip **c. un**bolt
b. unusual **d. un**dress

Page 24

1 amazement handful penniless fondness

2
move → ment
tear → ful
hope → less
sad → ness

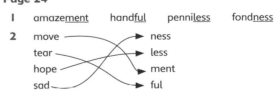

Page 25

1   It was the smallest kitten in the basket.

2   clean**er**   build**er**

Page 26

1   **a.** rejoined
     b. hopping

2   Accept any word from the same word family for example
     a. unhappy
     b. sadness

Page 27

1   He is **moving** house next week.

2

Present tense	Past tense
I drip	I **dripped**
he **drips**	it **dripped**
we are **dripping**	they **dripped**

SPELLING

Page 28

1   **a.** W<u>e</u> went to the b<u>ea</u>ch to s<u>ee</u> the sand.
     b. The ch<u>ie</u>f raised the gr<u>ee</u>n flag complet<u>e</u>ly.

2   **a.** fright   **b.** cube   **c.** shield

Page 29

1   **a.** taught
     b. Dinosaurs
     c. crawl

2   **a.** I cuddle my teddy <u>bear</u>/bare in bed.
     b. We picked pairs/<u>pears</u> off the tree.
     c. He went <u>upstairs</u>/upstares to fetch his book.

Page 30

1   **w**rite   **k**nob   **w**hole   **k**nife

2   knit, wreck, knock, white

Page 31

1   The dog ran **quickly** through the woods. (Also accept any other adverb containing *qu*.)
     In the **alphabet** g comes after f.

2   Accept any appropriate sentences using the given words, for example
     We made a **graph** of our favourite foods.
     It was very **quiet** this afternoon.

Page 32

1   **a.** camel   **b.** capital   **c.** squirrel

2   tow**el**, hospit**al**, bott**le**, pup**il**

Page 33

1

after a short vowel sound	after all other sounds
ledge badge dodge	page charge

2   **a.** stage   **b.** large   **c.** strange   **d.** judge

Page 34

1

Word	Split into parts	Unusual spelling patterns
friendly	friend+ly	ie making short e sound
behind	be + hind	ind
improve	im + prove	o–e making oo sound
people	peop+le	eo to make ee sound le at the end

2   Accept any appropriate sentence using each word, for example:
     a. I told the **others** there was no football.
     b. We learned our spellings **because** there was a test.
     c. They folded their **clothes** neatly.

Page 35

1

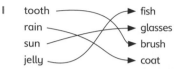

    tooth → glasses
    rain → brush
    sun → fish
    jelly → coat

2   Accept any appropriate compound word, for example:
     a. moon**light**   **c.** tea**spoon**
     b. wheel**barrow**   **d.** bed**room**

Page 36

1   **a.** there   **b.** their   **c.** they're

Page 37

1   **a.** sale   **b.** meet   **c.** paw

2   Accept any appropriate sentence using each word, for example:
     a. The **sun** is very hot.
     b. His **son** is good at football.

Page 38

1

Singular	Plural
window	**windows**
kiss	**kisses**
church	churches
flower	flowers
toe	toes

Page 39

1   **a.** trays   **b.** ladies   **c.** lorries   **d.** keys   **e.** flies   **f.** berries

2   **a.** Lots of **turkeys** are sold at Christmas.
     b. We walked through several **valleys** before reaching the village.
     c. Some **countries** are often hot.

READING

Page 41

1   fiercely

2   ripped

3   *quickly* or word with similar meaning

Page 42

1   The teacher met them at the door. → 1
     Ralf held his mother's hand tightly. → 2
     Some of the children started running around near Ralf. → 3

Page 43

1   They were more difficult **or** she had to learn by using the easier things first **or** the balls were too easy.

Page 45

1   headings, subheadings

2   headings → the order things are done
     subheadings → what the whole piece of writing is about
     numbers → what is needed, but not the order
     bullet points → what a part of the writing is about

3   Shopping list

4   Because the order you do things in is important or similar answer.

1   It is about running or similar answer.

2   Mandalay or similar.

3   Accept any explanation that gives reasons for the choice.

4   Deep in the Jungle: Everything is about the jungle. There are huge trees, thick rainforest and a fast-flowing river.
    Exploring the Amazon: The story is all about someone making their way through the jungle towards the River Amazon.

1   Bella, Cheryl, Donna, the bus driver

2   **1.** Donna and Cheryl stayed to help the driver.
    2. Bella called an ambulance.

1   Accept any **two** of the following:
    Shannon is a town in Ireland.
    It is named after a nearby river.
    It has an airport.

2   The writer likes snakes.
    Snakes are warm and dry.

1   Accept any of the following:
    Nasreen is very funny.
    She makes everyone laugh.
    Everyone is happy when Nasreen is here.

2   It was quiet.

1   Tigers can run fast and have sharp claws and teeth.

1   (Lorna was) going very fast on her bike.
    (She) needed to stop quickly.
    There was a loud snap
    her front brake fell off!

2   She won't stop **or** She will crash or similar answer.

1   It has fallen out of a hole in Ethan's pocket or similar answer.

2   He has put his finger through the hole or similar answer.

1   **a.** walk, talk
    b. fun, run

2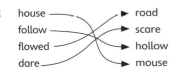
    house ⟶ hollow
    follow ⟶ mouse
    flowed ⟶ road
    dare ⟶ scare

1   rapid, runners, raced, ran

1   popped, whooshed

Notes

Revision planner

Grammatical words

Punctuation

Vocabulary

Spelling

Reading